THE HISTORY DETECTIVE INVESTIGATES

LONDON

Claudia Martin

Published in paperback in 2017
by Wayland

© Hodder and Stoughton 2017

ISBN: 978 1 5263 0185 7

10 9 8 7 6 5 4 3 2 1

Wayland
An imprint of
Hachette Children's Group
Part of Hodder & Stoughton
Carmelite House
50 Victoria Embankment
London EC4Y 0DZ

An Hachette UK Company
www.hachette.co.uk
www.hachettechildrens.co.uk

Printed in China

Produced for Wayland by:
White-Thomson Publishing Ltd
www.wtpub.co.uk

Editor: Claudia Martin
Designer: Clare Nicholas
Consultant: Philip Parker
Proofreader and indexer: Izzi Howell

Picture Acknowledgements

The author and publisher would like to thank the following for allowing their pictures to be reproduced in this publication:
Alamy: 7b (Rolf Richardson); **Bodleian Library:** 10b; **British Library:** 9; **Stefan Chabluk:** 4r, 15t; **Corbis:** 4l, 14 and 17t (Heritage Images), 10t (Chris Hellier), 11 (145/ Grady Coppell/Photographer's Choice RF/Ocean), 17b (Stefano Bianchetti), 24b (A.J. Sisco/Reuters); **Getty Images:** 20t (De Agostini), 25 (Planet News Archive); **William Hogarth:** 16; **iStock:** cover top (Juergen Sack), 2 (Ziva_K), 6 (JoanneatFuturespace), 13 (nicoolay), 19t and 26b (Deejpilot), 26t (Peter Zelei), 27 (dinosmichail), 29 (oversnap); **Kempes Nine Daies Wonder:** 12b; **Library of Congress:** 29b; **London Underground:** 21; **Mariordo:** 5; **Mary Evans:** 18, 20b (Illustrated London News Ltd); **Numisantica:** 7r; **Thomas Abel Prior/Musée d'Orsay:** 19b; **Shutterstock:** 1 (Alexandra Thomson), 8l (Fedor Selivanov), 8r (Pack-shot), 12t (Kamira), 15b (Cedric Weber), 22 (Everett Historical), 24t (mikecphoto); **Thinkstock:** cover main (pcruciatti); **US National Archives and Records Admin.:** 23t and b; **Yale Center for British Art:** 28.

Above: The London Underground sign was designed in 1908.

Previous page: Completed in 2012, the Shard is 309 m (1,016 ft) tall, making it the highest building in the United Kingdom. In front is the Millennium Bridge, opened in 2000.

The History Detective Investigates

Ancient Egypt
Ancient Greece
Ancient Sumer
Anglo-Saxons
Benin 900–1897 CE
Castles
The Celts
The Civil Wars
Early Islamic Civilization
The Indus Valley
The Industrial Revolution
Local History
Mayan Civilization
Monarchs
The Normans and the Battle of Hastings
Post-War Britain
The Shang Dynasty of Ancient China
Stone Age to Iron Age
Tudor Exploration
Tudor Home
Tudor Medicine
Tudor Theatre
Tudor War
Victorian Crime
Victorian Factory
Victorian School
Victorian Transport
The Vikings
Weapons and Armour Through the Ages

CONTENTS

When was London founded? 4

Which king first ruled from Westminster? 6

Who built the Tower of London? 8

Did Dick Whittington exist? 10

How did Tudor Londoners have fun? 12

What was the Great Fire? 14

Who were London's first police officers? 16

What was the Great Stink? 18

Why was the Tube important? 20

What happened in the Blitz? 22

Who is a Londoner? 24

Is London still changing? 26

Your project 28

Glossary 30

Answers 31

Further information 31

Index 32

Words in **bold** can be found in the glossary on page 30.

The history detective Sherlock Bones will help you to find clues and collect evidence about London. Wherever you see one of Sherlock's paw-prints, you will find a mystery to solve. The answers are on page 31.

WHEN WAS LONDON FOUNDED?

In 43 CE, the Roman army invaded Britain and set about conquering its tribes. Within six years of their arrival, the Romans had started to build a town on the north bank of the River Thames. They called their town Londinium, perhaps after the local words for 'river town' (*llyn don*) or – some people think – for 'fierce' (*londos*).

When the Romans arrived, the Thames Valley was scattered with villages of the Catuvellauni and Regnenses tribes. They used the river for water, fishing and **trading**. The Romans saw the area's potential. They founded Londinium where the Thames was narrow enough for a bridge but deep enough for a port. They soon built a wooden bridge across the river, roughly where London Bridge stands today. Before long, ships were sailing from the North Sea into Londinium's docks from Italy, Spain, Greece and Egypt. They brought wine, delicious fish sauce and olive oil. They loaded up with British silver, oysters and woollen cloaks. The Romans built roads to link Londinium with other towns in their new **province**.

🐾 **Which modern London street takes its name from the Roman wall?**

▼ This 2nd-century CE statue was found on the site of the Temple of Mithras. It shows Mithras, a Persian god around whom a new religion grew up in the Roman Empire.

▼ Today's City of London, a major financial centre, is on the site of Londinium. Some modern streets get their names from the six gates in the Roman city wall: Ludgate, Newgate, Aldersgate, Cripplegate, Bishopsgate and Aldgate.

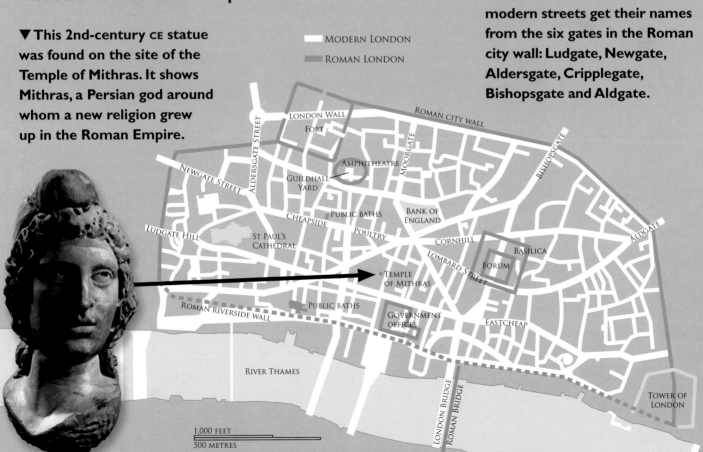

- ⬜ MODERN LONDON
- ⬛ ROMAN LONDON

LONDON WALL FORT · ROMAN CITY WALL · ALDERSGATE STREET · NEWGATE STREET · MOORGATE · AMPHITHEATRE · GUILDHALL YARD · BISHOPSGATE · CHEAPSIDE · PUBLIC BATHS · BANK OF ENGLAND · LUDGATE HILL · ST PAUL'S CATHEDRAL · POULTRY · CORNHILL · BASILICA · ALDGATE · LOMBARD STREET · FORUM · TEMPLE OF MITHRAS · ROMAN RIVERSIDE WALL · PUBLIC BATHS · GOVERNMENT OFFICES · EASTCHEAP · RIVER THAMES · LONDON BRIDGE · ROMAN BRIDGE · TOWER OF LONDON

1,000 FEET
500 METRES

Soon after Londinium was founded, the city met with the first of many catastrophes. In 60 or 61 CE, Boudicca, queen of a British tribe, burnt Londinium down. But it was quickly rebuilt. By 100 CE, Londinium had around 25,000 to 30,000 inhabitants. They were Romans, British people and foreign traders, drawn to the opportunities the city offered. The city was made the capital of Roman Britain, taking over from Colchester, in modern-day Essex.

▼ **Around 200 CE, a wall was built around Londinium's landward side to protect it from attack. Sections still stand today. A riverside wall was built after 280 CE.**

DETECTIVE WORK

Find out more about daily life in Londinium. Go to www.museumoflondon. org.uk and type 'Roman London' in the Search box.

Londinium's largest building was its three-storey **basilica**, where the city's governors and judges worked. It overlooked the forum, or marketplace. To the northwest was the fort, home of the city's soldiers. There were luxurious public baths, where people washed, exercised and chatted. On public holidays, cheering crowds watched gladiators fight at the amphitheatre. Londinium's inhabitants could make offerings at several temples, which were dedicated to gods such as Jupiter and Mithras.

The Roman historian Tacitus (c.56–c.120 CE) wrote about Boudicca's attack on Londinium and the fate of the citizens who did not run away:

'For the British did not take or sell prisoners… They could not wait to cut throats, hang, burn and crucify…'

WHICH KING FIRST RULED FROM WESTMINSTER?

The Roman Empire weakened and started to fall apart. By 410 CE, the last Roman soldiers had left Londinium. Abandoned, the city fell into ruins. Then, after 450 CE, the next wave of invaders arrived: the Anglo-Saxons, from modern-day Germany, Denmark and the Netherlands. It was an Anglo-Saxon king, Edward the Confessor, who made Westminster famous.

The **Anglo-Saxons** did not want to live among Londinium's ruins, so they started a little settlement on the riverbank just to the west. They called it Lundenwic ('London trading town'). The town grew to be home to 12,000 traders, craftspeople and farmers. By the 7th century, the townspeople had become Christians. They built St Paul's Church, probably on the site of today's St Paul's Cathedral.

DETECTIVE WORK

Explore Anglo-Saxon London through artefacts held at the British Museum. Go to www.britishmuseum.org and type 'Anglo-Saxon London' into the Search box.

▼ This reconstruction of an Anglo-Saxon village shows what ordinary homes looked like in Lundenwic. They were built from wood, with thatched roofs.

During the 9th century, Lundenwic suffered raids by **Vikings**. The Anglo-Saxon king Alfred the Great moved the town inside the Roman walls for protection. The walled city was now called Lundenburh ('London fort') and Lundenwic was renamed Ealdwic ('old trading town'). That area of London is called Aldwych to this day. King Alfred united southern England under his rule. As Alfred's successors took control of the rest of England, Lundenburh grew to be the largest city in the kingdom. Yet it still had to share the role of capital with the city of Winchester.

In 1042, Edward the Confessor inherited the English throne. A very religious man, he started to build a magnificent **abbey** 3 km (2 miles) to the west of Lundenburh's walls. Known as Westminster Abbey, it was on the site of today's famous abbey, which was rebuilt in the 13th century. Beside his abbey, Edward built a palace where he could hold court. It was Edward's grand building projects that established Lundenburh as England's most important city. Even today, England's parliament meets in the Palace of Westminster, on the site of Edward's palace.

The Life of King Edward, written by a monk in around 1067, tells us how Edward the Confessor chose the spot for his abbey and palace:

'*...it lay hard by the famous and rich town of Lundenburh and also was a delightful spot, surrounded with fertile lands and green fields and near the main channel of the river, which bore... wares of every kind for sale.*'

These coins were made in Lundenburh during the reign of Edward's father, Aethelred the Unready.

▼ **Sewn in the 1070s, the Bayeux Tapestry tells the story of Edward the Confessor's death and what followed. In this section, Edward's body is carried to Westminster Abbey for burial, after his death in January 1066. The abbey had not yet been completed.**

🐾 **What is being installed on the roof of Westminster Abbey?**

hIC PORTATUR: CORPVS: EADWARDI: REGIS: AD: ECCLESIAM: SCI PETRI APLI

WHO BUILT THE TOWER OF LONDON?

When Edward the Confessor died in January 1066, he had no children to take the throne. His brother-in-law Harold was crowned king, but was soon under attack from Edward's cousin, Duke William of Normandy, often called William the Conqueror. It was William who built the Tower of London.

DETECTIVE WORK

Discover who was imprisoned in the Tower of London at:
www.hrp.org.uk/
TowerOfLondon/stories

The White Tower still stands at the heart of the Tower of London. Later kings added more buildings to the castle, along with stone enclosing walls and a moat.

▼ This statue of William the Conqueror is at Falaise in Normandy, France, William's birthplace.

William was a descendant of Viking settlers on the northwest coast of France, and he spoke a type of French. His people were called **Normans** (from 'north men') and their homeland was Normandy. William and his army landed on the south coast of England, defeating King Harold at Hastings. Then they marched on London: William knew he had to control London before he could control England. London's citizens battled the invaders, but were forced to surrender. On 25 December 1066, William was crowned king in the brand-new Westminster Abbey.

The Normans' arrival did not greatly change life for ordinary Londoners. Yet they did not welcome their new rulers, with their different language and laws. William knew he had to protect himself and keep Londoners in their place. Straight away, he ordered the construction of three castles in London: Montfichet's Tower and Baynard's Castle (both now demolished) and, in the southeast corner of the city walls, a castle that became known as the Tower of London.

The first castle keep (central tower) was wooden, but it burned down in 1077. William ordered the replacement to be stone. The result was the White Tower, the first stone keep in England. It was designed to be a constant reminder to Londoners of the strength of their rulers. It was built of bright, cream stone from Normandy. Its highest defences overlooked the city itself. Its entrance was on the first floor, reached by a wooden staircase that could be removed during an attack. Around the tower were ditches and earth mounds, topped by wooden spikes. Inside, the tower was fitted out comfortably for William to live in when visiting London. There was also accommodation for prisoners.

The Norman priest William of Poitiers (c.1020–90) recorded William the Conqueror's life story. He wrote about the Tower of London:

'Certain fortifications were completed in the city against the restlessness of the huge and brutal populace. For [William] realized that it was of the first importance to overawe the Londoners.'

◄ This 15th-century illustration of the Tower of London shows Traitor's Gate (centre front), which was added in 1275–79. London Bridge can be seen in the background.

🐾 By which mode of transport did prisoners enter the Tower of London through Traitor's Gate?

DID DICK WHITTINGTON EXIST?

Most people know the story of Dick Whittington from pantomimes and folk tales. The real Richard Whittington was born in Gloucestershire, England, in the 1350s. He did become Mayor of London, not three times as in the story, but four times.

Richard Whittington's father was a **knight**, but not wealthy. When Richard was in his teens, he was sent to London to be apprenticed to a mercer. Mercers **imported** luxury cloth such as silk and velvet. They **exported** English woollen cloth. As an **apprentice**, boys (and occasionally girls) lived with a master of a trade, while learning the skills of the job. Masters had to be members of their trade's **guild**, or club. Among the most important guilds were the mercers, fishmongers and goldsmiths. The guilds controlled trade. They also governed the city and elected the Mayor of London from among their members. In the Guildhall, guild members met in the Common Council to discuss the city's issues.

▼ This medieval illustration shows a master baker with his apprentice.

DETECTIVE WORK

Find out more of the truth about Dick Whittington. Go to www.learningzone. cityoflondon.gov.uk/ schoolmate/City/sm_city_ stories.asp and click on 'Dick Whittington'.

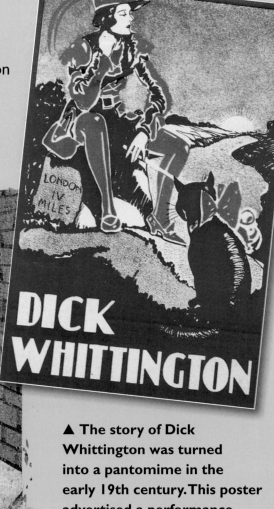

▲ The story of Dick Whittington was turned into a pantomime in the early 19th century. This poster advertised a performance in London in 1930.

When Richard had finished training, he became a master of the mercer's guild. Before long, he had made so much money that he was lending it out, even to the king. In 1385, Richard was elected to the Common Council. In 1397, he was elected to the highest post: Mayor of London. His job included acting as a judge in the courts, and speaking up for London to the king.

Like in the story, Richard married a girl called Alice FitzWarin. They had no children, so when Richard died he left his money to charity. It paid for work on hospitals, prisons and an almshouse, which provided homes for the poor. It was these good works that made Londoners start to tell stories about Richard. They probably mixed up the real story with a common folk tale about a poor boy with a magical cat. Perhaps 'Dick' Whittington's story stays popular because it tells us that anyone can make it big in London. That hope has drawn people to London for nearly 2,000 years.

A traditional rhyme tells us how a young 'Dick' Whittington walked away from London, only to hear the bells of the church of St Mary-le-Bow call him back:

'Turn again, Whittington, Thrice Mayor of London.'

The outline of which circular Roman building is marked on the paving stones of the Guildhall's courtyard?

▼ **In his will, Richard left money for improvements to the Guildhall, the meeting place for London's guilds.**

HOW DID TUDOR LONDONERS HAVE FUN?

When Henry VII, the first Tudor monarch, took the throne in 1485, London had around 60,000 inhabitants. From across Britain and Europe, more and more people flocked to London during Tudor times. The crowded city offered countless places to have fun, from theatres to bear rings.

For centuries, Londoners had enjoyed the religious plays put on in churches and at festivals. During the reign of Elizabeth I, plays became more varied, exciting and beautiful. Great playwrights such as William Shakespeare and Christopher Marlowe were working in London. The first **purpose-built** theatre opened in Shoreditch in 1576, north of the city walls. Theatres had to be outside the city limits, because the authorities disapproved. Many other theatres followed, particularly across the river in Southwark. By 1595, 15,000 people were visiting the theatre every week.

▼ In 1600, the famous actor William Kempe entertained Londoners by dancing through the streets.

▼ In 1599, the Globe Theatre was built in Southwark by Shakespeare's theatre company. The theatre was reconstructed in 1997, near the site of the original theatre.

In 1599, the Swiss traveller Thomas Platter (1574–1628) visited London. He wrote:

'Thus daily at two in the afternoon, London has two, sometimes three plays running in different places, competing with each other, and those which play best obtain most spectators.'

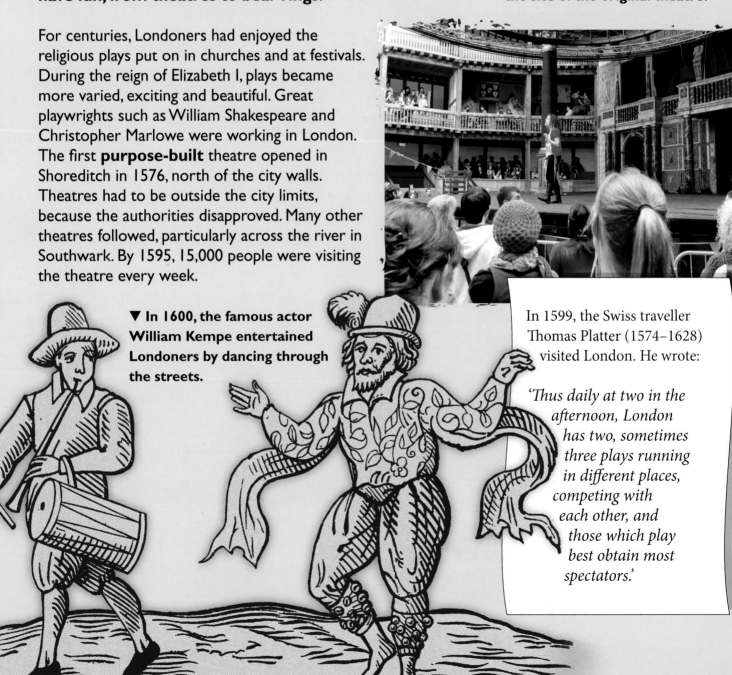

Londoners enjoyed the sight of blood. They rushed to cock-fights and to bear and bull rings, where the animals were set on by dogs. Like theatres, these buildings were often on the south bank of the river. When a criminal was to be executed, people queued through the night to get the spots with the best view. Football was often played on the open ground at Smithfield. The games were so rough that injuries, and even deaths, were common.

Shops and markets filled London's streets. Even London Bridge was lined with shops. After 1571, wealthier people could buy wigs, perfumes and feathers at the Royal Exchange, which was London's first shopping mall. Many times a year, Londoners enjoyed fairs, festivals and parades. St Bartholomew's Fair was held every August at Smithfield, with food stalls, jugglers, musicians and wild animals.

Yet many Londoners feared the crowds at public entertainments, because of the risk of catching plague, **sweating sickness** or smallpox. Such diseases were so common that a Londoner's **life expectancy** was only about 30 years old. The last major outbreak of plague in London was in 1665–6. It took the lives of 100,000 Londoners, about a quarter of the population.

DETECTIVE WORK

To find out more about the history of London's theatres, try the website of the Victoria and Albert Museum: www.vam.ac.uk/page/t/theatre-and-performance

▼ **This map shows London in 1572. London Bridge is still the only bridge across the river. Grand houses line the Strand, which runs from Westminster (far left) to the city.**

In 1572, **which places of entertainment were on the south bank of the river?**

WHAT WAS THE GREAT FIRE?

For years, people had predicted that London would burn down. Fires had destroyed parts of the city before. In 1665, the King himself, Charles II, wrote to the Mayor about the fire risk of London's wooden houses with upper storeys overhanging the narrow streets. In September 1666, the predictions came true.

The summer of 1666 was long, hot and rainless, so the city's houses were as dry as firewood. The riverside warehouses were packed with **flammable** alcohol, oil, coal and timber. Soon after midnight on Sunday 2 September, a fire broke out in an oven in Thomas Farriner's bakery on Pudding Lane, close to the river. The family escaped from an upstairs window, but their maid was too frightened to leave. She became the fire's first victim.

A strong wind spread the flames quickly from building to building. There was no fire brigade so neighbours and **parish constables** used buckets and hand-operated water pumps to fight the fire. Their job was made more difficult by crowds fleeing the city. The Mayor hesitated to order the usual plan of creating firebreaks by pulling down buildings in the path of the fire. By midday, the King himself had sent the order, but the delay left the workers struggling to get ahead of the blaze.

Samuel Pepys (1633–1703) was Chief Secretary of the Admiralty. Today he is most famous for his diary, in which he gave an eyewitness account of the Great Fire. On Sunday 2 September 1666, he wrote:

'*...it made me weep to see it. The churches, houses, and all on fire and flaming at once; and a horrid noise the flames made, and the cracking of houses at their ruins.*'

Which London landmark was destroyed on Tuesday 4 September?

This painting shows a view of the fire from a boat near the Tower of London (on the right) on the night of Tuesday 4 September. People are loading their belongings onto boats.

▼ **This map shows the area destroyed by the Great Fire. The easterly wind drove the flames westward.**

DETECTIVE WORK

Take a look at evidence about the Fire of London: www.nationalarchives.gov. uk/education/resources/ fire-of-london

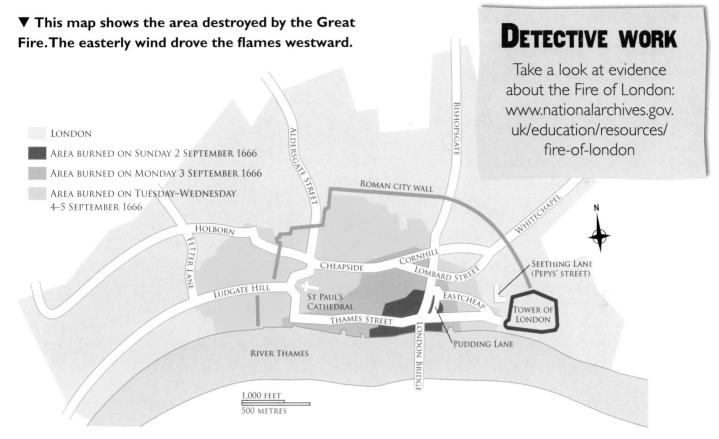

LONDON

AREA BURNED ON SUNDAY 2 SEPTEMBER 1666

AREA BURNED ON MONDAY 3 SEPTEMBER 1666

AREA BURNED ON TUESDAY–WEDNESDAY 4–5 SEPTEMBER 1666

ALDERSGATE STREET

BISHOPSGATE

ROMAN CITY WALL

WHITECHAPEL

N

HOLBORN

FETTER LANE

CHEAPSIDE

CORNHILL

LOMBARD STREET

SEETHING LANE (PEPYS' STREET)

LUDGATE HILL

ST PAUL'S CATHEDRAL

EASTCHEAP

TOWER OF LONDON

THAMES STREET

LONDON BRIDGE

PUDDING LANE

RIVER THAMES

1,000 FEET
500 METRES

At last, on Tuesday night, the wind died down. By dawn on Thursday 6 September, the fire was finally put out. The fire had left 100,000 people homeless. London's greatest church, St Paul's Cathedral, was destroyed, along with 87 other churches. Only four deaths were recorded.

Rebuilding began in 1667, after new **regulations** had been agreed: houses must have outer walls of brick rather than wood. Grand new street plans were rejected, because Londoners needed to rebuild their homes and businesses as quickly as possible. However, pavements and sewers were added, and major streets were widened.

▶ **Designed by the architect Sir Christopher Wren, the new St Paul's Cathedral was completed in 1711. Wren also designed 51 other churches to replace those burnt in the fire.**

WHO WERE LONDON'S FIRST POLICE OFFICERS?

Eighteenth-century London was a dangerous place. The city's narrow streets were teeming with tricksters, pickpockets, robbers and murderers. There was no organized police force to keep them in check. A man called Henry Fielding decided that had to change.

There were good reasons for the high level of crime. London did not have enough jobs for its 700,000 inhabitants. There was little help for the poor, apart from charity and workhouses. In workhouses, the city's very poorest lived and worked in grim conditions. Many poor people turned to alcohol, particularly gin, to drown their sorrows. The law was harsh: even minor crimes were punishable by death or **transportation**. For that reason, juries did not like to find people guilty of crimes such as theft, so many thieves were sent back onto the streets.

DETECTIVE WORK

You can read first-hand accounts of 18th-century crime and punishment on the British Library's website: www.bl.uk/georgian-britain/articles/crime-and-punishment-in-georgian-britain

Until now, Londoners had relied on parish constables and watchmen to patrol the streets. Sometimes, horseback patrols tried to catch the highwaymen who bothered travellers on the roads towards London. All these men were poorly paid, disorganized and untrained. Nicknamed 'Charleys', watchmen were often teased or even attacked.

◀ In this 1751 print, called *Gin Lane*, the artist William Hogarth shows what he believed were the effects of drunkenness among London's poor: crime, despair and early death.

Which cheap alcoholic drink was William Hogarth very worried about?

Henry Fielding was an author and London **magistrate**. In 1748, he came up with a plan for London's first organized police force. The result was a small group of trained officers, partly paid for with public money. Londoners called them the Bow Street Runners, because they were based at Bow Street magistrate's court. For the first time, there was someone to properly investigate crimes. From then on, the policing of the city grew more organized and respected. Finally, in 1829, the **Home Secretary** Robert Peel set up a large force to police the whole of London: the Metropolitan Police, based in Scotland Yard, in Westminster. Even today, you may hear police officers being called 'bobbies', after 'Bobby' Peel.

▶An 1804 cartoon shows a wealthy Londoner between two quick-handed pickpockets.

◀The Bow Street Runners are arresting the Cato Street Conspirators, who plotted to kill the prime minister in 1820. One officer died during the arrest.

In 1751, Henry Fielding (1707–54) wrote about the difficulty of catching criminals in the huge, bustling city:

'[London] appears as a vast wood or forest, in which a thief may harbour with as great security, as wild beasts do in the deserts of Africa...'

WHAT WAS THE GREAT STINK?

I n the summer of 1858, London faced another catastrophe. The River Thames had been smelly for years, but the hot weather was making the stink unbearable. The reason was simple: the river was filled with human sewage and factory waste. The disaster was called the **Great Stink**.

London had an old, leaking system of sewers, which dumped the city's human waste (urine and excrement) straight into the Thames. Most **Victorians** thought the smell of the sewage could spread disease. They blamed the smell for three outbreaks of **cholera**, which had killed 31,000 Londoners. In reality, it was not the smell but bacteria in the sewage that was causing the problem. Polluted water was piped from the Thames straight to the public pumps from which many people took their water.

In summer of 1858, an article about the Great Stink appeared in the *City Press* newspaper:

'*Gentility of speech is at an end – it stinks, and whoso once inhales the stink can never forget it and can count himself lucky if he lives to remember it.*'

▼ **This cartoon was drawn during the Great Stink. It shows the River Thames introducing his horrifying 'children' to a female figure who represents London. The lady looks like Queen Victoria.**

🐾 **Which diseases did the Victorians think they could catch from the Thames?**

DIPHTHERIA.   SCROFULA.   CHOLERA.

FATHER THAMES INTRODUCING HIS OFFSPRING TO THE FAIR CITY OF LONDON

(*A Design for a Fresco in the New Houses of Parliament.*)

The windows of the elegant new Palace of Westminster, home of the nation's parliament, faced right onto the river. All the curtains were doused in chloride of lime to block out the stink. Not surprisingly, parliament swiftly made a law to raise money for new sewers. In 1859, a massive plan was put into action, masterminded by the engineer Joseph Bazalgette. Over 2,000 km (1,250 miles) of new sewers were built to carry sewage safely through the city and far down the Thames, so it could be flushed out to sea.

The Victorians made other great improvements to their capital city. They built new schools and hospitals, as well as 18 bridges across the Thames. They created parks, such as Victoria Park in east London, so Londoners had places to relax. In 1851, Queen Victoria's husband, Prince Albert, helped organize the Great Exhibition in Hyde Park. With the money raised by the exhibition, land was bought in nearby Kensington. Here museums, colleges and a concert hall were built, including the Natural History Museum, Science Museum, Victoria and Albert Museum and the Royal Albert Hall.

▲ **Work on the current Palace of Westminster began in 1840, after the old palace was destroyed by fire. It was designed by Charles Barry and Augustus Pugin.**

▼ **The Great Exhibition was held in a purpose-built hall called the 'Crystal Palace'. There were exhibits of sculpture, machinery, photography and the world's largest diamond.**

DETECTIVE WORK

Examine pictures and plans of the Great Exhibition on the website of the Victoria and Albert Museum: www.vam.ac.uk/page/g/great-exhibition

WHY WAS THE TUBE IMPORTANT?

Between 1800 and 1900, London's population rose from 1 million to 6.2 million people. The city centre grew more overcrowded than ever. It became essential to build new homes in the villages and countryside around London. The London Underground rail network, often called the Tube, played a key part in the city's expansion.

In the 1830s, the new above-ground steam railways started to link London with other towns. London saw a growing number of commuters, people who lived outside London and worked in the city. Then, in 1863, the first section of Tube line opened. It ran beneath London's busy streets to link the railway stations of Paddington, Euston and King's Cross with the **financial centre** in the City of London. It was the world's first underground railway. It carried 38,000 passengers in its steam trains on the first day. Today that section is still part of the Metropolitan Line.

As more Tube lines were constructed, businesspeople and builders worked alongside. They bought land around the new stations and built street after street of homes. The city spread, with villages expanding to meet towns and becoming **suburbs** of London. Posters, poems and songs advertised the delights that awaited Londoners if they moved to the suburbs.

▲ This 1908 London Underground poster advertised the newly developed suburb of Golders Green. It shows a spacious home, green space and attractive lifestyle.

DETECTIVE WORK

Explore how Tube travel has changed by examining the objects at the London Transport Museum: www.ltmcollection.org/museum/index.html

◄ A 1934 cartoon shows a Tube station with business-people on the right platform and holidaymakers on the left.

Some suburbs were built to be affordable for workers. For example, Walthamstow, developed in the 1890s, offered small **terraced** homes. Later, leafy outer suburbs were built for wealthier Londoners: Pinner, developed in the 1920s and 30s, offered **semi-detached** homes. Many poor Londoners had to stay where they were, in the cramped inner city.

The arrival of the Tube, along with motor buses after 1902, also changed how Londoners spent their leisure time. At weekends, East Enders could quickly and cheaply reach Epping Forest on the line known today as the Central Line. Daytrips were organized by factories, churches, pubs and workhouses. To give everyone a good time, teashops, donkey rides and boating lakes opened.

A 1925 London Underground poster advertised moving to the northern suburb of Edgware:

'There dwelt a man in the City of London, but the fogs and smoke thereof did cause him such ill-ease, that he said unto his wife, My love, let us adventure unto Edgware and there buy us an house out of income.'

▼ **By 1908, when this map was printed, London had 8 underground lines. Today there are 11 lines and 270 stations.**

🐾 **Which central London station (which has since closed) was named after a famous museum?**

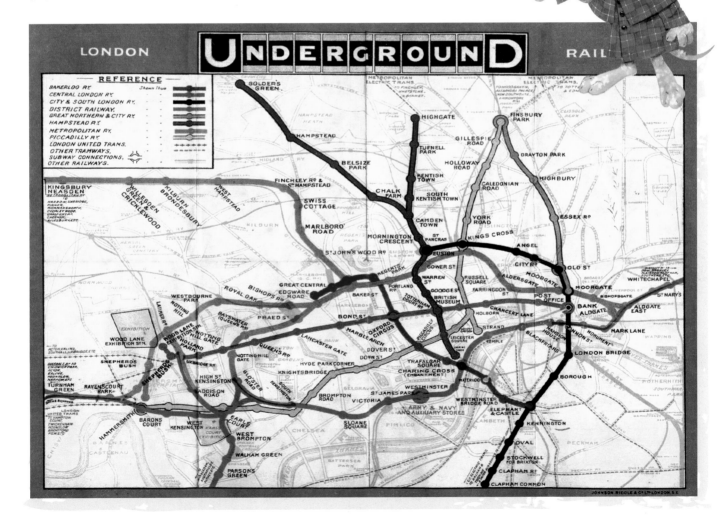

WHAT HAPPENED IN THE BLITZ?

Between 1939 and 1945, the world was plunged into World War II. Britain and its allies battled against Germany and its allies. The Blitz took place between September 1940 and May 1941, when 30,000 tons of explosives were dropped by German planes on London and 15 other British cities. Blitz means 'lightning' in German.

The Blitz destroyed over 1 million London homes and killed 20,000 Londoners (20,000 people were killed in other British cities). London took the brunt of the bombings, particularly its East End, which was close to the important docks. The aim of the bombing was to destroy British industry and wear down the British people into surrendering. Although factories were destroyed, the Blitz did not greatly damage British industry. The bombing only seemed to make Londoners more determined to win the war. Even today, people talk about the 'spirit of the Blitz' when Londoners show bravery in the face of danger.

The bombing of 29–30 December 1940 was so ferocious it was called the Second Great Fire of London. Firemen battled to save St Paul's Cathedral from the blazes. This photo became a symbol of London's unbreakable spirit.

When Buckingham Palace was hit by bombs, Queen Elizabeth (mother of Queen Elizabeth II) said:

'I'm glad we've been bombed. It makes me feel I can look the East End in the face.'

DETECTIVE WORK

Find out how Londoners behaved during the Blitz on the website of the Imperial War Museum: www.iwm.org.uk/ history/the-blitz

When German planes were spotted approaching London, the air raid sirens were sounded. People raced for cover in their cellars, under their stairs, in home-made bomb shelters or in public shelters. Around 1 million children and some of their mothers had been **evacuated** to the countryside for safety. Yet many families had chosen to stay together in London. In their shelters, people sang songs, played instruments and told jokes. People listened to the bombs falling, as a direct hit was likely to be fatal. After the all-clear siren, Londoners came out to help the injured and look at the damage. Fire crews complained about nosy crowds as they tried to put out the blazes caused by fire bombs.

On 8 May 1945, Germany surrendered. In London, the church bells rang out in celebration as everyone took to the streets. All day and all night, strangers linked arms to dance, sing and laugh together.

▼ **In September 1940, these East End children agreed to pose for a photographer in the rubble of their home.**

▼ **Londoners pass the time in a public shelter during the Blitz.**

🐾 **Which underground structures were often used as shelters during air raids?**

WHO IS A LONDONER?

London has always been a city of invaders and immigrants. Today more than 300 languages are spoken in London. Over a third of Londoners were born outside the United Kingdom. Most Londoners say that anyone who lives in London is a Londoner.

By the early 20th century, London had large Chinese, French, Irish, Italian and Jewish communities. Many were drawn by the trading opportunities in London. Others hoped for safety from religious persecution. The Protestant **Huguenots** fled from Catholic France in the 17th century. Many of London's Jews fled Eastern Europe in the late 19th century. Yet, at first, each group of arrivals faced distrust or even attack. Eventually, each in their turn was accepted, and added their own stamp to the city: Huguenot silk-weavers, Jewish synagogues, Italian restaurants, Chinese festivals.

▲ There are more than a thousand curry houses and stalls in London. Most of them are owned by the Bangladeshi community.

 In which famous square are London's Chinese New Year celebrations held?

▼ Londoners gather to celebrate Chinese New Year.

In 1948, the British government passed the British Nationality Act. It gave the right to live and work in Britain to all citizens of Commonwealth countries. These countries were part of, or had been part of, Britain's **empire**, including Jamaica in the Caribbean; India and Pakistan in Asia; and Somalia and Kenya in Africa. The aim was to attract people to work in Britain's public services, such as the National Health Service.

In April 1948, an advert was put in a Jamaican newspaper offering cheap fares to London for anyone who wanted work. Around 490 people took up the offer. They travelled on a ship called the *Empire Windrush*.

▲ The *Empire Windrush* arrived in London's docks on 22 June 1948. Most of the passengers were men.

DETECTIVE WORK

Examine documents and photographs about the *Windrush* and its passengers at: www.nationalarchives. gov.uk/education/resources/ bound-for-britain

Like new **immigrants** before them, many arrivals on the *Empire Windrush* met with rudeness and, occasionally, violence. However, most of them found work and settled in the city. Over the next decades, they were joined by tens of thousands of other Commonwealth citizens. Many people also arrived from countries such as Poland, Portugal and Turkey. In 1966, London's Caribbean community started the Notting Hill Carnival. Today it is London's most popular festival, with a million Londoners of all backgrounds partying on the streets every August.

Lucile Harris was one of the few women to travel from Jamaica on the *Windrush*. She said:

'*...anybody come to this country they can make a good life, it's a nice country, it cold, it's different, but you can live happily...*'

IS LONDON STILL CHANGING?

London has always had to change in order to prosper and grow. Today, the city still adapts to meet the changing needs of its 8.6 million citizens. In the 21st century, London is still a magnet that draws people, wealth and skills from across the world.

For nearly 2,000 years, much of London's wealth came from its docks. The goods being imported and exported changed over the centuries. By the mid-20th century, exports included Hoovers, radios and cars, made in London's factories. But by the 1980s, the noisy docks had moved out of the city towards the sea. Today London's income is £300 billion a year, with only £8 billion brought in by the docks.

There are also very few factories left in London. Instead, the city gets most of its money from **service industries**, such as banking and tourism, and creative industries, such as fashion design, film and technology. As it has been for hundreds of years, the City of London is one of the world's major financial centres. Finance is so important to London that, since the early 1990s, the industry has spread into a second district, in the old docks: Canary Wharf.

▲ **Picnickers relax in Greenwich Park. Over the river is Canary Wharf, one of London's two financial districts.**

DETECTIVE WORK

Find out how London's homes have changed over the last 400 years: www.geffrye-museum.org. uk/explore-the-geffrye

Can you spot any London landmarks, old or new, in this photo?

London's skyline constantly changes as new constructions reach for the sky. This photo shows the City of London and the old dock area.

Boris Johnson, Mayor of London from 2008 to 2016, said:

'[London is] a city whose energy conquered the world and which now brings the world together in one city.'

London's population is set to reach 10 million by 2030. Today the city's greatest challenge is to provide enough houses, hospitals and schools, without destroying green spaces. Solutions include building in disused industrial areas, taller buildings, and future developments well outside the city boundaries, perhaps on the Thames **estuary**. To cut back on pollution and meet the demands of its 3 million commuters, London also needs to improve its public transport.
A £15 billion new train line is under construction: Crossrail, which will run east to west across the city from 2019.

Like Dick Whittington in the story, people from all over the world are still drawn to London, hoping for success. Yet Londoners have not lost their appetite for fun. When they are not hard at work, they can be found in the city's markets, theatres, festivals, stadiums, parks and museums.

▼ **Londoners and tourists watch an acrobat in Covent Garden market, where Anglo-Saxon Lundenwic once stood.**

YOUR PROJECT

Now you know about London's eventful history, it is time to put together your own project. Perhaps you could do some detective work about the subject that interests you most. Maybe it will be one of the many catastrophes to hit the city, from plague and fire to the Great Stink or the Blitz.

If you were interested by Samuel Pepys' first-hand account of the Fire of London, try writing your own diary about an important moment in London's history. Imagine you are an eyewitness to Boudicca's attack on Londinium, the Norman invasion or the opening of the first Tube line. Write about what you can see, hear and smell. Samuel Pepys wrote that the fire made him 'weep'. How does your event make you feel?

If you live in London or close enough to visit, take a tour of your favourite building. Perhaps you could choose a landmark like Buckingham Palace, Westminster Abbey or the Tower of London. If a tour in person is not possible, take a virtual tour on the Internet. Then create a model of your building or make a poster or book. Think about who constructed your building and why. What great events has your building witnessed?

Another idea for a project is to pretend you are a journalist who has been sent back in time to interview your favourite London character. Maybe it will be Richard Whittington, Henry Fielding or someone who has just arrived on the *Empire Windrush*. What questions will you ask?

▼ Between the 16th and 19th centuries, the River Thames sometimes froze in winter. 'Frost fairs' were held on the ice. Write a diary entry about visiting this 17th-century fair.

Project presentation

- First of all, research your project carefully. Visit your local library and the school library to find books about your subject. If you live near London, visit a museum or take a walking tour.

- You will find a wealth of information about London on the Internet. Put together a list of useful websites: include museum websites, websites for great buildings, and some that include stories about famous Londoners.

- To illustrate your project, print out pictures of objects, paintings and places that you find on the Internet. Buy postcards from the museums you visit. You could also do drawings of people and events that you find on websites.

▶ Try basing your project on this photograph, which was taken in 1890–1900, looking down Cheapside from St Paul's Cathedral. The black and white image was coloured with inks. Imagine you are one of those pedestrians. What do you see and hear?

▲ You could decide to do your project about Buckingham Palace. The building was begun in 1703, but did not become the main royal home until 1837.

GLOSSARY

abbey A building where Christian monks or nuns live.

Anglo-Saxons The people who ruled England from about 450 until the Norman invasion in 1066. Many were Angles, Saxons and Jutes, from modern Germany and Denmark.

apprentice A person who is learning a trade from a skilled employer.

basilica A large building used by the ancient Romans as a public meeting place and courts of law.

cholera A disease that causes vomiting and diarrhoea.

empire A number of provinces or countries ruled by one leader or group.

estuary The wide mouth of a river where it nears the sea.

evacuated Removed from a dangerous place to a safer one.

exported Transported goods to other countries so that they can be sold.

financial centre An area with many important banks and businesses.

flammable Easily set on fire.

guild A group of merchants or craftspeople, formed to protect their interests.

Home Secretary The member of the United Kingdom's government who is in charge of law and order.

Huguenots Protestants who fled from Catholic France during the 17th century. Protestantism and Catholicism are branches of Christianity.

immigrant A person who comes to live in another country.

imported Brought goods into the country from abroad.

knight A low member of the land-owning nobility.

life expectancy The average age to which a person is expected to live.

magistrate A low-level judge.

Normans A Viking people who settled in northern France in the 10th century.

parish constable An unpaid, elected official who helped to police London from the Middle Ages until 1829.

province Area of an empire with its own government.

purpose-built Designed specially for a particular use.

regulation A rule or law set down by the government.

semi-detached Joined to another house on one side.

service industry A business that offers a service (such as transport or entertainment) rather than makes goods.

suburb An area in the outer city where people live.

sweating sickness A deadly disease that struck Europe between 1485 and 1578. Modern doctors are not sure exactly what it was.

terraced Joined to other houses in a row.

trading Buying and selling goods or offering services.

transportation Being sent to work in an overseas colony as punishment.

Victorians People who lived in Britain during the reign of Queen Victoria (1837–1901).

Vikings Peoples from modern Denmark, Norway and Sweden who raided and settled across Europe from the 8th to 11th centuries.

ANSWERS

Page 4   The street London Wall, on the site of the fort, is named after the Roman wall.
Page 7   A weather cock is being put in place. This was probably the artist's way of showing that Westminster Abbey was not completed when Edward died.
Page 9   Prisoners entered Traitor's Gate by boat.
Page 11   The Guildhall was built on the site of the Roman amphitheatre. Its shape has been marked on the courtyard's paving stones.
Page 13   On the map, two rings for bear- and bull-baiting can be seen on the south bank.
Page 14   St Paul's Cathedral burnt down on Tuesday 4 September 1666.
Page 16   During the first half of the 18th century, William Hogarth and many others were worried about gin: on average, Londoners drank 10 litres (2 gallons) per person per year.
Page 18   The diseases ('children') in the water of the Thames were thought to include diphtheria, scrofula and cholera. In reality, only cholera is caught from polluted water.
Page 21   British Museum station, on the Central London Railway (today called the Central Line) closed in 1933.
Page 23   Tube stations were popular shelters during the Blitz.
Page 24   Trafalgar Square hosts London's Chinese New Year festivities.
Page 26   From left to right, you can see Tower Bridge (1894) and the skyscrapers nicknamed 'The Walkie-Talkie' (2014), 'The Cheese-Grater' (2013) and 'The Gherkin' (2003).

FURTHER INFORMATION

Books to read
Explore!: London by Liz Gogerly (Wayland, 2015)
An Infographic Guide to London by Simon Holland (Wayland, 2016)
Truth or Busted: The Fact or Fiction behind London by Adam Sutherland (Wayland, 2012)

Websites
www.fireoflondon.org.uk
www.ltmuseum.co.uk
www.museumoflondon.org.uk
Note to parents and teachers: Every effort has been made by the publishers to ensure that these websites are suitable for children. However, because of the nature of the Internet, it is impossible to guarantee that the contents of these sites will not be altered. We strongly advise that Internet access is supervised by a responsible adult.

Places to visit
British Museum, London, WC1B 3DG
Globe Theatre, London, SE1 9DT
London Transport Museum, London, WC2E 7BB
Museum of London, London, EC2Y 5HN

Natural History Museum, London, SW7 5BD
St Paul's Cathedral, London, EC4M 8AD
Science Museum, London, SW7 2DD
Tower of London, London, EC3N 4AB

INDEX

Numbers in **bold** refer to pictures and captions.

Alfred the Great 7
Anglo-Saxons 6–7, 27

Bayeux Tapestry **7**
Bazalgette, Joseph 19
Blitz, the 22–23, **22**, **23**, 28
Boudicca 5, 28
Bow Street Runners 16–17, **17**
British Library 16
British Museum 6, 21, 31
Buckingham Palace 22, 28, **29**

Canary Wharf 26, **26**
Charles 11, King 14
City of London 4, 20, 21, 26, **26**
crime and police 16–17, **17**
Crossrail 27

disease 13, 18

Edward the Confessor 6, 7, **7**, 8
Empire Windrush 25, **25**, 28
entertainment 12–13, **12**, 21, 25, 27, **27**, **28**

Fielding, Henry 16, 17, 28

Globe Theatre **12**, 31
Great Exhibition 19, **19**
Great Fire of London 14–15, **14**, **15**, 28
Great Plague 13, 28
Great Stink 18–19, **18**, 28
Guildhall 10, 11, **11**
guilds 10, 11

Hastings, Battle of 8
Hogarth, William **16**
homes **6**, 15, **20**, 21, **23**, 26, 27
Houses of Parliament 7, 19, **19**

immigration 4, 6, 8, 12, 24–25, 27
Imperial War Museum 22

London Bridge 4, **9**, 13, **13**, **14**, 28
London Transport Museum 20, 31

markets 5, 13, **24**, 27, **27**
Marlowe, Christopher 12
Mayor of London 10, 11, 14, 27
Millennium Bridge **1**, 2
Museum of London 5, 31
museums 5, 6, 13, 19, 20, 21, 22, 26, 27, 29

Natural History Museum 19, 31
Normans 8–9, 28
Notting Hill Carnival 25

Palace of Westminster 7, 19, **19**
parks 19, **26**, 27
Pepys, Samuel 14, 28
population 5, 6, 12, 13, 20, 24–25, 26, 27

River Thames 4, **14**, 18–19, **18**, **26**, 27, **28**
Roman wall **4**, **5**
Romans 4–5, 6
Royal Albert Hall 19

St Paul's Cathedral 6, **14**, 15, **15**, **22**, **29**
Science Museum 19, 31
Shakespeare, William 12
skyscrapers **1**, 2, **26**
suburbs 20–21, **20**

theatres 12–13, **12**, 27
Tower Bridge **26**
Tower of London 8–9, **8**, **9**, **14**, 28
trade 4, 6, 10, 26
Trafalgar Square **24**
Tube (London Underground) **2**, 20–21, **20**, **21**, **23**, 28

Victoria and Albert Museum 13, 19
Victoria, Queen **18**, 19
Victorians 18–19
Vikings 7, 8

Westminster 6, 7, **7**, **13**, **19**
Westminster Abbey 7, **7**, 8, 28
Whittington, Richard 10–11, **10**, 27, 28
William the Conqueror 8–9, **8**
Wren, Sir Christopher **15**